In the Soup

John Calderazzo

In the Soup

© 2025, John Calderazzo

Books may be purchased in quantity and/or special sales by contacting the publisher. All inquiries related to such matters should be addressed to:

Middle Creek Publishing & Audio 9161 Pueblo Mountain Park Road, Beulah, CO 81023
middlecreekpublishing@outlook.com
(719) 369-9050

First Paperback Edition, 2025
ISBN: 978-1-957483-36-8

Cover Photo: Phil Benstein.
Cover Design: David Anthony Martin, Middle Creek Publishing & Audio.

Author Image Credit: Stephanie G'Schwind.

In the Soup

John Calderazzo

Middle Creek Publishing & Audio
Beulah, CO   USA

Contents

3 Windy Day at the Dump

In the Soup

I pulled the tab on a can of turkey noodle soup,
& the trapped air sighed. I was glooping the contents
into a pot when I heard it sigh again. Stuck to the bottom
was a ball of noodles, which began to move.
A miniature man, sitting cross-legged, stared out
at me as he rolled some stiffness from his shoulders.
He wore noodle-colored robes & looked like
Mahatma Gandhi, with a shaved head & those
rimless glasses. He wasn't the least bit smeared
with soup. Had he been meditating in there, protected
by a bubble of antediluvian peace & willpower?
It felt odd to imagine him, a vegetarian, biding
his time among the turkey chunks. So, Venerable
One, I asked, does all this meat floating around
bother you? He shrugged. *You do what you have to do.*
And what is that? I said. *Keep coming back*, he said.
*The Great Wheel. You never know how these things will
shake out.* I wanted to believe him but was troubled
by the fact that the pull tab had not been invented
when he died in 1948, hammered into silence
like his brothers in non-violence, MLK, Jesus.
Boy, it would be good to see those guys coming
around again on a carousel, jumping off to lock
arms with Gandhi, the three of them brimming
with their short-lived superpowers of peaceful
resistance. As though reading my mind on the pull

tab problem, he said, *This is not my first*
merry-go-round, you know. Which made me
wonder how often he'd come back over the years
to stand up to the multiplying nightsticks of tyranny.
Maybe Gandhi was one of those comets
that swing by every few decades to inspire us
before looping out again to refuel with light &
direction. Without a bullet to his name, he'd out-
thought the entire British Empire. Just then,
my wife called from down the hall to ask how
the soup was coming. *Well, you have things to do,*
Gandhi said. *Good to see your mindfulness starting*
in the kitchen. Next time you drop a pebble into a pond,
follow the ripples if the cause is right. I resolved right
then to spend many fewer hours watching Netflix.
I might even unretire from the world, stroll out into
some shouting. Gandhi asked me to take the can
outside & lay it on its side. He had places to go.
You don't by any chance have a cat, do you?
No cat, I said. That guy, always thinking.

1
Big Day

Second Coming

Something drew me outside, a whisper
from the fading stars. Feathers floated

down, gray, cinnamon-rose. They
swayed, spiraled, slashed. I looked up,

but saw no leaden cumuli of birds,
just a snowfall of feathers in growing

light. I plucked one from the faintly
hissing air: tail feather, passenger pigeon.

Such an odd name for a bird, as if
the millions that once blocked the sun

had booked passage on steam trains
bearing down on oblivion, the birds

packed in wing to folded wing, rocking
together on seats, arm rests, luggage

railings, rush-hour commuters cooing
under little black bowlers, tiny briefcases

packed with memories of wolf howl,
unshackled river & grizzly roar.

The feathers came down for hours,
mounded over Adirondack chairs,

puffed from the saxophone my next-
door neighbor was playing in his backyard,

practicing the blues. His tone deepened.
Feathers re-leafed winter cottonwoods.

Limbs of chinkapin oaks three states
over bowed to earth, as they once did

under birdstorms beyond imagining.
Oceans turned sludge gray, cinnamon-

rose. Even the wind-bitten crew of
the farthest-out whale boat, preparing

to gun into silence the sunken canticles
of the sea, began to comprehend
what we had done.

The Retired Professor Reads in the Library

Sitting cross-legged on cool linoleum amid windfall books,
I'm turning pages, old-time reporter's notebook open beside me.

I've been here for hours. If someone were to push a button,
would these high-tech shelves begin to hum & close me in?

Well, I'm not all here, anyway. Last week, two floors down
in the bedrock level veined with Latin American literature,

I pulled down books & fell in with Quechua poets, whose
pages sang me back to a high valley in Peru I'd hiked to

a few months before, where I looked up & cheered young
men dressed as bears who'd been battling demons all night

on a glacier. Law students, taxi drivers, shopkeepers
from Cusco had climbed for hours under bitter stars.

Knee-deep in snow, they were planting crosses taller
than themselves & dancing between crevasses that

hadn't yet learned their names. At 17,000 feet, I shook
with cold & ached for breath among thousands of pilgrims,

staring at those moon-shouldered warriors. *Qoyllur Rit'i*,
ancient sky ritual, a fluted chat with rueful mountain gods

I mostly failed to understand. Plucked last week from
their basement shelves, the poets shook off dusty sleep

& opened themselves to me, offering insights after the fact.
Today, I'm trying to wring light from science—rising

CO2 levels, acres of disappearing ice pack the Andean
bear-men were fighting to preserve for their harvest.

Now I pull down books & lean back to let a student step by.
"Thank you, sir," he says, probably thinking, *Him again.*

The old guy. Shadowed with Earth-worry, I'm otherwise happy
as I was at ten, freed from class to roam the school library, a forest

of night things lit by fireflies. Soon, I hope to lift off & skywrite
my essay—dancers on star-crossed ice, snow hunger in the eyes

of mountain people. Someone who sleeps far from mountains
might read it one day & wake with the perfect verb to help

rivers keep blessing the corn. Meanwhile, O lucky me,
free to read until the day I'll sit still for so long in my

traveling that light sensors will fail to detect me,
& with a small hum a thousand books will seal me in.

Baby Breaks In

Suddenly an infant in the house, crawling
like mad over our childless habits, years

we sat motionless, reading, refrigerator
purring, heat from floor registers whispering

as though the furnace knew better than
to disturb us. But Baby doesn't care. He

pulls a shiny fist from his mouth, examines
it, scrambles to the great-aunt couch which

SueEllen never allows me to pile books on
or threaten with Cherry Garcia. He claws

himself to his feet, hangs on to a velvet
seat cushion, wobbles up down up, his

fourteenth predicament of the morning . . .
& *everything's fine*, SueEllen loves this,

she sweeps in to help him clamber up,
this bomb of a child, soft & dense as a bag

of flour. I lift him away, my hands slung
under his belly, he air crawls, hits the rug,

scoots for the shelf where the Oahu-blue
ceramic bowl sits beside the Persian vase

passed down through the forever of family
time. *Whoops*, says SueEllen, snatching them

away. *Time to child-proof!* His parents have
managed to cap the wall sockets. But what

will protect the fuse box, Baby's voltage
a threat to blow the system? Douglas

Joseph, DoJo for short, Zen name for
learning center, which he has become.

Who knew he could have such fun
slapping his way down the hall to push

the battery check button of the carbon
monoxide detector? *Beep!* DoJo gives me

his Curious George grin, tacks for the dog
door, dog long gone, cooling it in the safety

of the backyard. *Beep!* Now I'm walking with
him held to my chest, facing out the way

he likes, so he can flap his arms at the
world. When he cries, I hum into the top

of his warm head, his first words starting
to simmer in there. He calms & I sway

with him around the kitchen island. I can't
sing, but sing, anyway *Baby DoJo's rocking*

in a boat, boat's rocking in the sea, and oh
what a way to be. Now I hold him in autumn sun

at the picture window, house finch twitching
at the feeder. Now we watch a cloud reinvent

itself, cow to potato to jellyfish. DoJo's eyes
track wind-torn leaves. Now, only weeks later,

he's gone, family flown to his grandparents
in Peru, & *Beep!* here's a Crazy Guy alert,

silver-haired man wandering around the house,
squeezing a bedroom pillow to his chest,
humming into it, not knowing what else to do.

Circus Flyer

—East New York, 1965

Payday, fading winter afternoon, skylights the color
of dirty laundry. Sewing machines chugged down.
Women at long tables snapped off their lamps, easing
back from a week of fastening cross straps & straw
sunflowers to summer shoes. Laughter, bursts
of Spanish. The floor shuddered as a stamping
machine smashed out a final leather pattern. A pregnant
supervisor, Glory, rolled her neck & drifted to a window,
called down to her guy. We milled around, waiting
for our checks, when I noticed money changing hands—
a bet of some kind was on. In a swept space near
earthen mounds of leather, I watched tiny Pepe standing
alone. After a moment, he raised his arms & dove into
a handstand. A feathery bounce & he held it like iron,
did it again, one leg higher than the other. Smallest man
in the place, thin as banjo string, a gold tooth showing
when he smiled. Smaller than most of the women, too,
in their slender twenties, though he was older. All of us
breathing a marinade of leather & glue we carried home.
Most mornings, as I jogged down the steps of the el,
the train rumbling off, I could almost see a cloud of it
reaching out for me as the tilted-open factory windows
swung into view. In Puerto Rico, the story went, Pepe
had been a circus flyer, until the night he grabbed
nothing but air, the sawdust smashing up at him.

He lived with his sister's family, now, in Flatbush,
a sickening dip in his gait as he pushed shoe racks
between stations, stubby wooden wheels rattling
madly over floor beams so thick they must have come
from trees grown tall before the birth of time.
As he stood in late shadows, looking thoughtful &
shaking out his arms, a crowd gathered. Pigeons
scratched at the skylights & the last sewing machine
died. A chunky guy who liked to tease the Dominican
women made a show of crumpling a ten & placed it
on the floor. With no fuss, Pepe popped his handstand,
locked in above the money, the four-inch cuffs of his
jeans sliding halfway down his calves. He lifted away
his left hand, fingers open, as if signaling for quiet,
leaned right in counterbalance & levered himself down.
His arm muscles jumped like mice under his skin.
Dios mio, breathed the woman crushed in next to me,
one of the team that slapped glue onto cork heels.
Pepe didn't waver. He pursed his lips, kissed the ten,
pushed back up with half a day's pay in his mouth.
We whooped & stomped. Even the guy who'd lost
was laughing. Springing back to his feet, minus
the inverted grace of his handstand, Pepe almost
buckled, his bum leg folding in. He caught himself
& held up the ten. In the dimming light, his gold
tooth shone.

Lift Off

Waiting for my Ethiopian dark roast, I browse
the wall of flyers—whale song concert, yoga

in the park, empowerment talk: Don't Stew, Do!—
until I catch myself floating an inch or two

above the floor. Soon I've risen past the tabletops.
I look down at a bearded man who resembles

me, hunched over a laptop, bald spot revealing
his worry that he's outlived his two thimbles

of wisdom & must try to compensate by
typing furry stanzas of monkey Shakespeare.

My head bumps the filigreed tin ceiling, roar
of espresso machines hissing down to a hush

of starfire as I slip through the roof, through
basketries of contrails. Achieving orbit, I revolve

in a spacesuit & watch a banyan tree drift by
with its standing army of roots, looking like

its picture on the milk carton I studied last week
while doing not nearly enough to quell the muzak

of chainsaws. The roots become tentacles of a giant
squid whose plate-sized eye, in which I regard my

Downward Dog floating self, regards me back.
A gray whale, belly stuffed with cephalopod beaks

& eyes, comes hungering in, singing an infinitude
of yearning. The Library of Alexandria rises

from the earth, my beckoning having lifted it
away from the word-burners of history,

who curse up at me. *So there!* I shout back,
recalling my reflection in the squid's eye.

White-robed scholars standing on the library steps
applaud & offer me a peek at a lost play of Sophocles

& 17 of Sappho's 10,000 un-sung lines. Good thing
I've just learned Greek. The scholars look amazed

when I mention that one of Sappho's peaches
could be a stand-in for a breast, a body-song

bursting under the un-returnable gaze of the sun.
They ask me to explain more, so impressed are they

by my MFA in Creative Meandering.

But I'm growing tired, caffeine needy,

& someone seems to be calling me, saying, *Sir?*

You want that dark roast with room for cream, Sir?

Waking from an Afternoon Nap

The hiss of the shower draws me
into the rainforest of the bathroom.

Behind steamed glass,
SueEllen's smudged body sways.

She's crying again, remembering
her parents, recently gone,

& her kid brothers, David
then Doug, retired from lives

in difficult tropical places,
gone, too, in their sixties,

just three years apart,
their families still bashed.

She's likely sitting again
on the family couch, a little girl

holding Doug in his hospital blanket,
feeling his important breath

float up, his eyelashes so long
that years later they'd swipe

the insides of his glasses.
I want to give her time to let

the orchids of her grieving
bloom. But the steam teases places

in my lungs I haven't felt in years.
I imagine a green tendril curlicuing

over the shower wall. I wait. I wait.
I slide open the glass door & slip in.

Returning to the Cloud Forest

—for Agustín

There I say pointing out the passenger window
first glimpse of the canopy-snagged
clouds the lounging rain
that's where I'll pull on rubber boots
cross the river on the swaying bridge
scan mud trails for the blue flame
of poison dart frogs
that's where I'll doze with hooting
night things lumbering fruit bats
where Agustín bent down
& scooped up a hummingbird chick
I might have stepped on
tiny as an emerald on your finger
he cupped it back to its nest
beneath woven oropendola flights
this man about my age
who'd learned to save the small
by saving himself as a child
stolen by people weeks downriver
then barely a teen made his run
his stashed canoe slipping through
a no-moon night the stars hushed
in the unfamiliar dialect of the river
& now his family his guests the trees
protected in the flower-scented air

angel's trumpet heliconia
his sly machete-trimmed trails
winding into dead-ends hiding his home
the waterfall you can't bathe under
until hours after rain the ceiba giants
greening the shivered light
leave me here please let me walk
the one true trail going in

Big Day

—Tahuayo River, Amazon Basin

The birds of the forest slept.
Honey creepers and flycatchers slept.
A pair of scarlet macaws, leaning into each other
on a limb, dreamed of arrowing side by side
over jungle canopy.
In its slumber, a horned screamer
made no sound.

The paradise jacamar slept,
its iridescence on hold until morning,
its name forming in the brain of the ornithologist
sitting on the edge of his bed,
lacing his boots by feel.

In the pre-dawn light of the jungle,
which was no light at all,
the great potoo did not sleep,
but might as well have.
Night bird masquerading
as a weathered piece of wood,
it stood motionless on a high limb,
withholding its haunting rasp.
The plum-throated cotinga slept,
and a razor-billed curassow with its beak of fire,
and a cock-of-the-rock with its body of fire.

Not a sound floated down from trees
with buttresses flung wide
to support this empire
of sleeping.
Eels slid through the river,
a tapir, a family of giant otters,
but orange-cheeked parrots slept hard,
and oropendolas tucked in their hammocky nests,
which hung over cove water near a dock
with a small motorboat,
which also slept.

Not a squawk fell
from the stars in their turning
over the winding mirror of black water.
Fed by Andes snowmelt
and long slopes of cloud forests,
the river widened through the jungle.
Birds with names plucked from jewelry boxes slept—
opal-crowned tanager, fiery topaz,
glittering-coated emerald.

In stick nests around a lagoon,
boat-billed herons, zigzag herons, rufescent tiger-
herons rose through gauzy sleep,
a capped heron ahead of them,
opening its bill as if to swallow the sun
as it rushed up through a roseate spoonbill dawn,

though dawn offered no hint
of arrival.

Bird names stirred the ornithologist's friend,
a local guide sitting slantways on a hammock,
cleaning his binoculars.
Names in English, Latin, Spanish,
a local dialect, reminded him
of one of the jungle stories of his childhood—
a harpy eagle, hunting for tree sloths,
sniffed trouble one day & swooped down
to pluck a bathing bride-to-be
from the river, before
demons disguised as pink dolphins
could lure her from the world of husbands.

Massaged by green air and the prospect
of so much naming, which was a kind of bird
chorus & balm for their souls,
the men felt their way
down the spongy plank steps
of the lodge built over water.
Each carried a thermos and sandwiches,
their unlit smart phones packed
with bird songs, mating calls, bird
images, bird behaviors.
Their eyes carried
bird beauty.

The ornithologist lowered himself
into the boat, his friend at the engine.
Overhead, a white-throated toucan
slept behind its beak.
The guide pushed off and pulled
the motor. On a limb across the river,
a spider monkey snapped awake, watching
in large-eyed silence, as the boat
purred off into sunrise.

The Secret Life of Mountains

—Front Range of the Rockies

A spring squall
smudges away
the wall of mountains,

Hallett Peak, Flattop,
granite domes & cliffs,
danger spires—

gone in a minute,
geology nothing
but breath.

Deep in,
a lupine meadow
scored with trails

softens, mists over,
dousing spot-fires
of glacier lilies.

Pasque flowers
close their petals
like eyelids folding

into meditation,
relieved from
the trespass

of cameras, boot
scrape, the beauty-lust
of hikers & drones.

Elk graze
untagged,
uncounted.

A moose,
large of belly,
rolls onto her side,

ready, finally
to push her calf
into the plush arms of fog.

Crossing the Ocean at Night

Half an hour in, I realize that
I've misplaced my glasses

in the baggage, my novel
& two magazines useless

as stones. How to pass the
time? Why not endow

the cabin ceiling with
titanium-attracting powers?

Leaning into the aisle,
in the bear-den gloom,

I imagine sleepers with
replacement knees & hips

slowly floating up from
their seats, straining at

their belts, some with knees
pulled up to their chests.

Next, I concentrate on the man
who's been hogging my armrest,

returning now from the restroom.
How puzzled he looks, scratching

the top of his head as an old
injury plate in his skull lifts

like revelation & clamps
itself to the ceiling,

him with it, his legs kicking.
Oh! he cries, almost in delight,

though not loudly enough to pull
the rest of us from our dreaming.

Diego in the Sky

It's come out of the mountains now
easing overhead flat-bottomed
sailing east towards the plains
not just the thunderhead itself
its slate-gray afternoon brow
& con man promise of Front Range rain
too many years & days of that above
sand rivers & rows of withered corn
but with a new mural billowing
up its side a mile high
rising as the cloud rises out of itself
like a kingdom of ideas
while down here re-imagining
the workaday nature of light
& mixing thunder & downpour tints
Diego Rivera thumbs the controls of
a thousand whirring paint-spraying drones

But Diego not entirely down here
positioned thirty feet above my backyard
chunky legs dangling from the platform
of my locked windmill as he examines
the entire canvas-flow of the sky
he's refused the harness I strap on
when I change the oil in the rotor box
but then he's Diego Rivera undeterred

by conventional storms of gravity
his last commission had him swaying
in fog from ropes on a redwood trunk
in California stroke by long stroke
brushing that giant
into background forest
disguising it from bounding wildfire
as the poets who winched him up
stood around & cheered

Thrilling to see him now at his control box
directing cloud sprayers to mural in
a gusher ten thousand buckets
of dripping black paint to inspire
more thunderheads to grumble & let go
to dream far more vertically
than dry lightning or the late-July
showers which seem to have
lost their way to Earth
wisping away into airy dementia
good to see his drone crew up there
moving with the cloud over the cracked
plains famished silos bony antelope
new grass dreaming beneath wizened grass
all of us looking up & waiting
for the first cold drops

Gravel Pit

For years as I drove by
following the wide meander of the river,
I admired the red farmhouse with two cars & a pickup
standing in a green army of corn.

Then one year the corn decamped.
Now & then I'd notice a wind-lifted roof shingle
sticking up, like a tiny door left open
through which a grown daughter or son
had flown, romanced off by some city.

Then it was just the pickup.
Then one day, beside the extinct silo
dabbed with swallow nests,
a shallow pit opened.

It was so sudden,
you'd think a saber-toothed tiger
had come sniffing down in the night
from the high country & clawed open the earth,
exposing the tumbledown mountain cobbles
in a prehistoric curve
in the river.

They were gold nuggets now
to the farmer or his widow,
retirement stones naked to the sky,
to be sorted & polished
to the speckled, river-bottom beauty
of dinosaur eggs, then trucked off & planted
on new lawns.

Then the pickup disappeared.
Soon, stone crushers & conveyer belts
moved into the pit, rumbling & clanking
all day & all night.

2
Gathering Voltage

Way Stones

1

A hiking friend has been knocking over
those fanciful slim rock piles you see
popping up in clumps alongside trails
in the wild. River cobble or red rock
vanity projects, he calls them, though
he rarely says much, just shakes his head
& kicks. Most don't stand long, anyway.
A season or two of crowbar ice & thaw,
wind horsebacking on wind, nosing
deer, microquakes from a realm deeper
than dream—they kick, too.

2

I don't mind them, myself. The best,
slender & elegant, suggest a tall dance
with gravity in the later style of Brancusi.
Or my spine. Not a bad reminder as I age.
If you hike in serious back country, though,
do not confuse them with old-time cairns,
laid down by travelers chastened by sly
mountains or baffling desert. The trail
goes this way, say those stones. Death
is that way.

3

On the thin-air pathways of the Andes

in Peru, every peak you see can be a stone-

faced God, every cairn an altar. Here's

a woman, baby on her back, herding

a cloud of alpacas. She pauses at an *apacheta*

whose shape echoes the ice-crowned peak

ahead. Is it rain she's praying for, lightning

mercy, the healing of an eye or heart?

A chance for her child to someday sit

in school? Here's a horseman, getting

on in years, packing the gear of trekkers.

He drifts off from the group & dismounts,

holds high a tiny fan of coca leaves, slips

it into a cairn crack. He needs no help

finding his way in these mountains. A last ride

through the stars is a different matter.

Under Mt. Ausengate

—Andes, southern Peru

In my dome tent, inside a down bag
inside another bag, I wake to the rifle
crack of a day-warmed glacier fracturing
half a mile above our camp. Only five
days hiking in these mountains, and I
know what comes next: the falling,
house-sized ice chunk scrapes and
splinters down a cliff face, in starlit
slow motion. It pounds the swollen
meltwater lake, which can't hold forever.
Long seconds, then a wave sloshes into
the far shore. In the village of river-
stone homes we tramped through,
just downhill, how many farmers
and herders are working a calculus
in their half-sleep—to move to the
creeping sand-dune slums of Lima,
which could soon enough bury their
children, or to live under this high-
country handiwork of the warming
skies, the lake finally bursting, in slow
motion, then an ice torrent jumping
with boulders, a rumble growing
in the night.

These Are the Beasts of the Earth, I Said

At the museum the other day I did a very good
bad thing, at least in my mind. I touched the art.
I couldn't help it, I widened my arms & lifted
a Jacob Lawrence print from the wall, part of his
"Genesis" series called "And God Created All
the Beasts of the Earth!" A late work, it features
a bearded preacher at his pulpit, muscular as
the Almighty, who resembles mid-career
James Earl Jones. Almost floating in blue sky
robes, he gestures to four open church windows,
guiding his congregation to behold the sixth new day
of Earth. One beast just sprung from his rock-
knuckled hands appears to be a black cat stretching
to become itself, & through another window
a shred of a bird claws into flight. I studied that
beautiful print with some dissatisfaction,
disturbed by the mildness of those creatures
despite their gyring Jacob Lawrence energy.
They seemed not nearly monstrous enough
for our times—for instance, a politely
cantering horse looks nothing like an
immolated steed of the Apocalypse. It's true
Lawrence is long gone, but we need a talent
like his to highlight the new ancient beasts that
walk the world these days. So I imagined
carrying that print across the gallery floor, then

holding it up to face a wall-bound piece that had
caught my attention minutes before. It was one
he'd completed fifteen years earlier, with the rage
of a younger man. "Confrontation on the Bridge"—
a Selma-inspired stand-off in which Black folks,
jammed on a bridge, grit their teeth in panic
at a horribly snarling dog, even as they refuse
to turn & run. I'm old enough to recall scenes
like that, Martin Luther King practically stepping
through our living room TV with so many others
in jackets & skinny ties, holding their ground
against the long-fanged police. Now *these*
are the Beasts of the Earth! I yelled, shaking
the Genesis print. Isn't this what a museum
should do, move us to autopsy history & ourselves,
urge us to walk stuff around the galleries, kick up
arguments among the displays to rearrange
our seeing? Don't we need more powerhouse
artists like Lawrence the Younger to come seething
out of his grave to inspire us, even as I know
he owes me nothing & the outraged best of him
should have moved us long ago to march out
of museums & stand down dogs whenever
we hear them snarl?

The Darker Moods of My Father

I'm growing nostalgic
for the darker moods of my father,
how he'd sit in our sunroom,
hunched forward in his bamboo chair,
growing silent in the black & white flicker
of the six o'clock news, his cigarette
hazing the last slant light of day,
my mother behind her book,
while longhaired mobs surged
across the screen against the war
no president or general could explain,
my own hair growing quietly against this thing
that wanted to cannon me into jungle mud
since the moment I'd turned eighteen,
old enough to pull a trigger
on a teenager crouched behind
a sweltering green wall, but too young
to vote on a reason for doing it,
my hard-charging factory-owning father
who hated institutions, priests
drunk on holy water, bureaucrats
who couldn't run a fever, as he'd grumble—
making my mother laugh—
he hated the waste & idiocy of it all,
but hated as much the grungy marchers,
&, later on, what he called the Nixon-hating

correspondents & op-ed writers,

until one smoke-filled evening, having sunk

into his shoulders, he muttered at the TV,

"Maybe the government should regulate

the damn journalists."

My mother shut her book

& said, "Oh honey, oh no . . . ."

& he instantly looked sheepish,

knowing he'd gone too far, back in those days

when it was still possible to go too far.

On the Subway

A lurch or two, & we slid from the grubby light
of the station, Queensboro Plaza or Hunter's Point.
Yellowed wall tiles & Broadway show posters
slipped back, blurring as we picked up speed.
Then tunnel dark slammed down. I rocked
beside my mother on the window seat
& stared out at a water pipe or covered electric
line—a python furred with dust, miles long,
wriggling up & down in triple time to sparks
& the squealing half-light from our passing.
When the doors whooshed open, the pipe had
disappeared, a snake waiting behind us
& up ahead, & I wondered what else was
moving through those dank places under the city,
maybe a man like the one who'd eyed me
through a hole in the bathroom stall at
the movies, or street bums, worn as creaking
shoe leather, just searching for a place to sleep,
their night-sized eyes helping them avoid
colossal cats or a hole that could pull them
into a sewer lagoon. My mother's bag pressed
between us, she gripped my left hand, her own
holding up her Daily News, fervid with mob
rub-outs, the story of a girl who'd sprinted from
kidnappers in Brooklyn. Amazing that she could
look so serene, my young blonde mother who

clipped tulips in our yard on Long Island,

reading now of a boy in the town next to ours

thrown by railroad tracks over the handlebars

of his Schwinn, unhurt but looking back at

his bike popping & melting on the third rail.

Teasing an Anvil Out of the Sky

One slow morning, I decide to tease
an anvil out of the sky. A trapdoor
in a cloud swings open & down
the anvil goes. Oh boy, soon it's dropping
so fast toward the red tile roofs
of an Italian hill town I didn't realize
was there that my mind has to jump on
a Vespa to keep up. I manage to make
the anvil sprout wings, though right away
I see they're the wrong size, wren feathers
on a bald eagle, so I hitch the dark iron
to a parachute which in my haste I've
stolen from a mouse-infested storage
unit. As a last resort, I try to build
a steel dome over the town's 16th century
chapel with its restored Titian. Before
I can finish, though, my imagination,
like an undertrained marathon runner,
hits a wall. The anvil punches through
the chapel & plunges most of the way
to Earth's core. It happens so quickly,
the old ladies in black at mass notice
nothing but the candles for the dead
shivering a little, then burning on.

Depression

1 Just Like That

When I was seized by it, struck dumb
by it as I stood at the counter in the bank,
the young teller, in a slate blue tie
turning eel black,
was holding out five or six
twenties. That seemed odd. I stared
at the ends of the bills, which were starting
to droop in his hand like peony stalks late in season.
I must have taken them & stuffed them in a pocket,
then waited for him to hand me something more,
maybe an instruction manual
for the rest of my life
or a map to my car in the parking lot.
That's how fast it came on.
See you next time, he said, looking at me hard.
There *will* be a next time, right?

For weeks, there was no time at all.
Or too much of it. The bedside clock
had fallen in love with itself,
hands turned to stone.
I managed to keep teaching,
the obligation & showtime of it powering me
through the final weeks of the semester,

though the students could tell.
In the hour between my Tuesday-
Thursday classes, I sat unmoving,
knees pulled up, in the womb under my desk.

At home, in bed or on
the couch, bright dim days of fog,
an hour lounging in every minute.
Now & again I blinked, as a dark-eyed junco
might dip for water at the bowl
on the picnic table,
lift its head, swallow its one drop,
pause to consider the chance of a hawk
swooping down. Did my eyes
ever really close?

Just months
before the moment at the bank,
I'd climbed a dazzling snow mountain
in Mexico, almost a mile higher
than our Colorado fourteeners.
Decades older than most
of my teammates, I felt like a moon
whose light you could read by, every sentence
a beauty.

Now, full eclipse.
Planets stalled in their grooves.

Sometimes, my wife walked

in. Walked out.

One fading afternoon, I felt

that she came in with God at her side.

Not an old man, He wore farmer's overalls

& a gimme cap, sat on the edge of the mattress

& willed me to float above the covers. He candled

my soul, then stared at me as He might

a cornfield shredded

by hail.

2 In the Snowy Range

A fire on the snow this morning—

a red-tailed fox staring at me across

the half-lit bowl of the valley. Minutes ago,

I squeaked along a ridge on snowshoes

as Medicine Bow Peak flushed pink

from top down. Below me, the fox cantered

over lake ice still in shadow. It zig-zagged up

a night-scalloped slope, dancing so lightly

in its private mind of snow I was surprised to

see it glance back at me & freeze. Descending

light turned its ears to points of flame.

Now its tail blazes up & I stare back.

I wonder if the snap & lick of its fire

will tell me what to do. For months, voices

shimmered out of hairline cracks in my day

& gave me advice I fought hard to ignore.

A runner splashing through rain as I drove by,

my windows up, invited me to jog with him

until our breathing merged & guttered out.

On a bike path in town, a fox sidestepping

out of cattails urged me to squeeze myself

into the fretless wool of its den. But not

this fox, blazing on snow in the subzero air.

It stares at me, it's true, but then shrugs off

across the slope & disappears over a hill,

taking fire & all my burning voices with it.

Fire Trout

—for Stephanie G'Schwind

They lazed in a light-filled pool, you said.
Facing upstream, they swam in place, their shadows
wavering on golden bottom sand, three trout massaged
by the sun-stained current flowing out of the forest.
Such clear long breath slipping through their bodies.
Watching, crouching among willows in the waterside
grass, you tried to keep your shadow to yourself.

I wonder, though, what happened when you turned,
half-standing suddenly as you saw the thin plume
rising from the nearby forest—the first minutes
of the firestorm that would incinerate lodgepoles
& crashing moose, choking rivulets & creeks
for months.

Did those trout startle too? Did they sense the long
black river growing inside their river, the freshly burnt
water pushing their way?

Sufi Tree

Late summer, Flattop Mountain at tree line,
I wade through krummholz to a scree field
clotted with gritty snow.
I approach the one trunk standing,
a corkscrewed limber pine, wind-sanded
& deeply scored, its stony wood the color of moonlight.

It's turned maybe three times in a century—
a slow-motion Sufi dancer.
Leaning against it,
I feel its dervish energy & lift my arms,
imagine spiraling & rising into an ecstasy of friends
scooped from their lives without warning.

My rock-fisted Uncle Clyde
nursing a beer at his kitchen table,
his eyes slipping shut, the saltshaker in his hand
spilling not a grain despite the sudden pull of the sea.
The neighbor girl, gone at 22, who sang
on summer nights to her horses.

So many gone or leaving
like snow spirits sublimating from these flanks,
light swept into greater light.

And me down here,

rooted as this tree, but hoping to spin & rise,

if only briefly, to walk & talk among them.

Kraken

—for Richard Jacobi

The emails & phone calls come more often now,
friends, cousins, neighbors our age, starting to fall,
ambushed by snow hiding driveway ice, ankle roll
on a friendly trail, knee buckling on vacation
cobblestones, concussion from wooden stairs
at home. A heater cord sent my friend
Vicki pitching over like a sequoia in her
living room. That's how she told it, amazed,
knowing she was lucky, no lung puncture
or cracked rib like her long-time guy Richard,
who chose unwise shoes to take out the garbage
& was slammed to stony ice. Today, a 40-second
video zips in from my tall nephew in Peru. His
one-year-old hauls himself up to stand free beside
a chair, plops right back down, rubber-boned,
with a bounce & a laugh. I laugh, too, even as I
sense what's reaching for him—gravity, the Kraken,
tentacled monster of the deep—already taking
his measure.

Gathering Voltage

Biking in the late-afternoon sun,
I near the crest of Bingham Hill,
prepare to step off, gulp water,
wipe my stinging eyes. I'll admire
the rough hay blanket of the valley,
snake-blaze irrigation ditches,
the maroon brick silo leaning
more each year, the eight ivory
horses browsing. Then I'll glide
home. But now I see coal-stained
clouds rushing in, then a bolt
of lightning.

Years ago, my brother-in-law Bruce
& I were climbing into a shadowless
stone world above tree line when
blue-black clouds came booming
over the summit. We ran, giant-
stepping down, Bruce hobbling
behind on bad knees. A cannon
shot made me flinch. Splintered
rocks clattered onto the scree
field between us. Bruce squatted,
still as a cairn. I forced myself
to crouch, crushed shut my eyes
under the fatal breath of the sky.

Never again, I told myself that
night, staring at the motel ceiling.

Now I'm creaking over this hill
on a metal bike, the sky rumbling.
I stomp on the pedals, tilt down,
crank into high, lean low, my wind-
breaker snapping, the air roaring
through vents in my helmet. Rain
begins to fling darts. The front
wheel hisses water into my face.
Shivering as I fly, I sense a lightning
bolt moving into position, gathering
voltage, checking its GPS, its terrible
book of names.

First Thing

Sunlight taps my bedroom window.
A man stands there in a battered

Yankees cap, staring in, homeless
or addicted, long-traveled.

He removes the cap, his head
steaming in the morning air.

His hands make a bowl that fills
with a glittering sea, which widens

& brims with lateen-rigged boats, like
the ones I saw off the coast of Zanzibar,

their sails pushing across the horizon
like fantastic tropical fish.

Now he cups a blood orange being
gnawed by one of the monkey kings

of China. In the sky over his shoulder,
a virga of macaws. Across a field, bison

chew through barbed wire, crunching
themselves back to the tallgrass prairie.

He holds out a fan of greeting cards:
Goya war prints. He offers me

a stapler to fix relationships,
a hammer to break them.

A woman I knew at the wrong time
appears by his side, looks into me

with unblinking chips of sky. Behind
me, a prayer wheel I didn't know

was bolted to my bedside table
begins to rumble, drowning out

my household gongs of doom.
Now he's fishing in his pocket

for something more.
I fling open the window,

as grateful for this bounty,
as amazed as I was the first time

it came to me more than fifty years
ago & almost every morning since.

Kayaking Flatwater

—Lake Irwin, 11,000 feet

We glide, almost dozing in the honey
of the sun, my aging dachshund Weasel
perched in my lap like a king.
Ahead of us, the surface riffles
like a delirium of fingerlings crowding up
for a peek at the sky—a breeze
that sweeps over us, prying at Weasel's
ears, trying to tell him something.
He tenses & trembles, yanks his leash,
paws the side of the cockpit, yips & bites
at slapping waves which darken his
snout & turn him into a pup again,
making me laugh. The wave-chop
re-muscles my arms, urges me
to paddle harder, bumping us along.
My ballcap flies off, but I don't mind—
we're boys, now, Weasel & I, gulping
mountain air. Only later, in the tent
speckled with stars, Weasel curled into
the bottom of the sleeping bag, do I feel
the sting of sunburn under the thin place
in my hair.

3
Windy Day at the Dump

Windy Day at the Dump

I walked to the back of my SUV,
yanked down my cap against wind

whistling up from sunken, gull-spattered
foothills of trash. The birds held their

places, buffeted on carpet mounds,
punched-in screen doors, box springs

shapeless from exhaustion. Beneath
this wind, another—a shush of far-gone

bamboo groves, bending teak forests
cut & hammered into chairs & tables,

wobbly, now, beyond repair. One
by one, I swung black plastic bags

into the maw, javelined a floor lamp
whose fizzing light had lent menace

to everything I'd been reading, even
comic novels. I waved at the caged-in

man on his mondo tractor, its steel-
spiked wheels jouncing over boulder

fields of bags. *Crunch!* An explosion
of pages, medical records of a last parent

to die, the draft of a youthful novel
too embarrassing to recycle, its nowhere

plot freshened & re-arranged by moving
air, letters from old loves, loosened

from a file cabinet of obsession or neglect.
Everyone, every old thing, plowed under,

mashed together. I reached for my
last item, an Audubon wall clock, a bird

painted at each hour, red-flecked house finch,
loon, oriole, songless for months in my

kitchen, a battery change failing to inspire
the hands to do more than twitch.

I wanted that thing as far from me
as possible, so I frisbeed it out. A gust

caught an edge & flipped it straight up,
its plastic face flashing in the sun.

Ten thousand gulls shrieked into flight.

70

Fourth of July

When the fireworks from town dim out,
our stars return. At our picnic table with couples
from Reno & Tampa, we're serving
strawberries with whipped cream.
When I hear a siren starting to race out
from town, I glance at SueEllen.
One wailing becomes two,
though nobody else seems to have noticed.
An ambulance, then a police car strobe past,
gunning it upcanyon, where
we know people.

Let it not be a bicyclist in a ditch,
helmet spinning away. Or a child immolated
by fever, or fire climbing from mouse-frayed
wiring behind a cabin wall.
Let it merely be water
broken in a first-time mother,
or a flatlander gasping for air.

Night hunkers down.
Listen, says somebody,
as the coyotes waiting patiently out of the light
start to call after the sirens.
Long-deaf little Otto, parked at my feet
for scraps, somehow knows to raise his snout & yip.

Suffering has been acknowledged. I bite into
my first strawberry, my teeth hurting
from the chill.

Late-Stage Capitalism

—Elk Mountain, Wyoming

Behind the cabin, my young niece Lea & I climbed
the bare hill, laughing, poking each other, but trying
not to crush the green shoots threading up through
snow-smashed mats of brown grass. As I heard
a small cheeping, Lea grabbed my arm & said, *Whoa!*
At our feet, a nest with four chicks, their trembling
beaks opened wider than their heads. Their tongues
were tiny arrows. Soon, they closed their mouths.
They were hairless, blue-veined, beautiful in their
baby alien ugliness. A coyote trotting by could eat
them in a gulp. I blocked the sun with my hand
& their mouths snapped open, the chicks frenzied
in the sudden shadow they thought was their mother.
Lea glanced at me. I saw that one was falling behind.
Soon they'd be scrambling over its shriveled body.
Which was next to be ravaged by the hawk beak
of supply & demand? I thought about explaining this
to Lea, when she said, *They're just baby birds. Maybe
we should leave them alone?* Eight or nine years
old & she knew exactly what to do. Hand in hand we
walked downhill. I just love learning from the young.

Highway Fool

—south of Cape Girardeau

No doubt unwise to have skidded
to a stop on the shoulder of this four-lane
Mississippi of concrete, eighteen-wheelers
slamming by, rocking my ticking car.
I open the door, calculate
an unfatal moment to sprint out &
stop a turtle's suicide crawl toward
water, its shell a dusty WWI helmet
powerless under the heavy artillery
of long haulers as it scrapes along,
sniffing the river, the actual Mississippi
sweeping behind the grass dike
running along the highway.
How often I'm numbed by the Big
Unsolvables, but this I can do.
I zip out, grab the turtle, heavier than
I thought, dash across the median
& two more lanes, & set it in knee-high
grass as a truck whomps by behind us.
It's pulled its legs inside the cave
of itself. I give it a nudge, think, Go,
a Heaven of Water awaits you.
Go & don't turn back.

Mouse Season

When the cold found our valley,
a mouse folded its origami bones
& slipped into the garage, leaving
its black seeds on my worktable.
In the late afternoon I found
one of last year's traps & set it
with a mash of white cheddar.
Barely dark when SueEllen
heard the snap & called down
the hallway. *Later*, I called back,
staying with my movie, letting
the mouse settle into its sudden
house of death. The least I could
do. Up to write at 4 a.m. but
writing nothing, I checked
the trap. A mouse lay beside it,
gray, white-bellied, not a whisker
bent. Stilled, it seemed, by the
grievous shock of the miss.
Hours later, I checked again.
No mouse. No cheddar. All
of this a week ago. I've yet
to reset the trap.

Little Boat

—Santa Cruz Island, California

Sometime in the night, I crawl from my tent
& drift through the campground under giant
eucalyptus trees, their papery bark peeling
away like book pages. The beam of my head-
lamp leads me past the lit rubies of island
foxes, until I stand shivering on beach
pebbles amid a ruckus of sand-crusted sea
kayaks, paddles, life jackets. Wetsuits hang
from a line, slack bodies whose souls have
slipped out to swim through the night—
comet tails of phosphorescence. I stand
until a spotlight rises & falls out on the water.
Tonight, it's furred, a glowing dandelion
in fog, distant but growing. A little fishing boat,
maybe, pilot crazy enough to have puttered
across the channel from Ventura between
thrumming cargo ships pushing their
private tsunamis. Or a woman at the wheel
of a stolen skiff, searching for her old
rhythms in the swell & tilt of the tide,
dolphins rising to greet her. Maybe a father
bending at his oars, trying to make something
right against the current. Every night,
I pass under the eucalyptus trees shedding
their groggy syllables of sleep.

I go down to the cold pebbles & stand,

sweeping my beam over the black water.

Third Bank of the River

I sit on a boulder along the pounding Poudre River
with my little grand-nephew DoJo, watching
an armada of yellow rafts bounce past,
then slalom single file through a dip in the rapids
where everyone lifts their paddles overhead, whooping.
Not a one notices DoJo waving madly, though I see
he's slid a few inches down the slope of our rock
towards slick moss.

I hook a finger through the belt loop of his shorts,
& we watch nothing but rock-broken current
until more rafts smash by, & among them
a wooden coffin so hidden in whitewater
I almost miss it. Minutes later, another coffin
bobs among rafters digging hard at the water.

Who knows why the dead are running this river—
maybe for a last thrill before the crushing silence
of the sea, or to prove they can still
flow among us when they wish.

DoJo's shorts tug at my finger,
so with my other hand I crumple the back
of his t-shirt & hold on for all I'm worth.

In My Sleep, I Become an Angel of Migration

And I rise from bed, and from my hall closet
I grab my cape of feathers and fly over
my backyard cottonwood with its hooting
great-horned owl and the peace that attracts
the owl. Tonight, I sail east, over the perilous
blue bend of the planet, to the Mediterranean
glittering between Africa and Italy. When I
find the first stick raft crammed with parched
families, the kind of raft you've read about,
forever taking on water, I call down in many
languages to say that Isola de Lampedusa,
the island the refugees fear might have sunk
under the weight of their desperation, in fact
lies just out of sight, like mercy, and I urge
the wind to stay its course, even as I know
that a broiling stone prison waits for those
families. Though better that than the cooling
dark at the bottom of the sea.

Learning to Meditate

Just close your eyes & breathe. Smile.
Think, *Welcome back, my old friend.*
Try not to slouch in your chair, though.
Let the big lozenge of the zafu tucked
behind you support your crunchy
spine, much as this circle of fellow
breathers will help calm your whack-
a-mole mind. Still, don't let everyone
cross the finish line of transcendence
ahead of you. Not that you're in a race.
But you're not a *loser*, either. Relax
the shoulders, but quit peeking across
the circle at the young woman whose
high cheekbones have made you recall,
for the first time in years, the bafflingly
nice girlfriend whom you failed to—
okay, stop! Dismount this thought-stallion
& walk it back to the present moment.
Breathe. Let the eyes fall closed. But
don't *scrunch* them, they're not iron
doors blocking out the clanging world,
which is but a zephyr, even as chaos
of your own making keeps hammering
your soul. The wall between in & out
will dissolve soon enough, like that
cheeseburger-shaped cloud you observed

this morning, rearranging itself into

a shaggy kangaroo, then wisping away,

as though the roo had ever so slowly

climbed into its own pouch. Admire

the cleverness of this simile. Now

chuck it into the ego dumpster. Exhale

all future admirers. Note how trying

not to think tends to invite your best

thoughts, which—too bad!—you need

to toss away. There's a *koan* for you.

Note also how the sunlight streaming

into the room has backlit your eyelids

to exactly the color of a saffron robe,

though no monk is running this show,

just a nice woman, probably born more

mellow than you'll ever be, who has

struck, three times, a bell of mindfulness

the size of a beachball. Try not to jump

to the future & imagine how truly

awesome it would be to strap on a

meditation tool belt, for those jangly

times *off the cushion*, as they say. Still,

how cool to thumb a teensy crater

into the dirt, then squirt it full

with a water pistol you've unholstered

from the belt, creating your own personal

lotus pond, which would ripple with

the song of a tiny bell unhooked from

your belt & struck with the handle of
your Swiss Army knife. Instant relief
from suffering! Note how escaped
parakeets on telephone wires are
celebrating your liberation by starting
to sway in cosmic harmony, as though
auditioning for some Bollywood . . .
Breathe, damn it!

Under the Windmill

I'm opening my laptop
for maybe the third time before 8 a.m.
when SueEllen walks in on me.
Again? she says. Close that thing!
Go outside & stare at . . .
a weed.

I give this some thought.
At the base of our four-story tall backyard
windmill, I find a spiny plant. Genus & species:
Weed. Its September leaves are straw.
It looks like it's good at being itself,
so I settle into lotus position
& give it a stare.

Above me, in no wind,
the great metal blades empty their minds.
After a time, in the dry breathing of the morning,
the weed trembles, an infinitesimal quake,
as if it senses a fault in the planet's crust,
not jumping, exactly,
but starting to think about it,
as birds, at the turn of
seasons, must shiver
for a moment when imagining

air maps unfolding ahead of themselves,
pond by shimmering pond.

Dear weed,
lanky Bodhisattva
standing outside the plashing
water park of Nirvana,
holding back to help the rest of us,
teach me to lift my eyes from my blue screen
to your sunlit body, to these metal blades waiting
for a creaking breeze to help them
lift water into the sky.

Backyard Crabapple

Just another tree
until limb-bending spring snow.

Then the pink explosion,
bright as any cherry blossom.

Then the bees arriving, inviting me
to duck under branches

& listen to 10,000 tiny
motorbikes, Kawasaki bees

zizzing
an inch from my ear.

Soon I'm flower-zonked,
like a courtier in the old

drinking game in which
you must write a *tanka*

before a paper boat
with lit candle & your name

circles back, making you
down another *sake,*

your friends cheering
& laughing

as your world tilts
& you fumble

for the proper
syllable count of praise.

Crazy Idea

—on the trail to Arthur's Rock

A hundred times I've hiked to this tallgrass
meadow, but never with such flowers ablaze,
following spring rains without end. Before me,
a sprawl of chest-high bee balm, dazzling
purple, fidgeting with bumblebees the size
of figs. I wade into the middle of it,
a great hum rising, & recall that you can
crush these blossoms to brew mint tea.
I stumble into a flattened round place
where deer must have settled in the night,
pressing into shape a living basket.
What if I could sit cross-legged here,
in late afternoon sun, with certain men
who've been convinced, somehow,
to put aside vengeance & the artillery of history,
to sip tea with each other & listen to the roar
of bees fade into the evening? What if we could
ease back onto the earth & shoulder to shoulder
watch the stars that watch us with their weary
eyes? Could we share this space until morning?
Not one of us would need to say a word.

Passing Through Wingo

Escaped from the mad highway,
we wriggle for miles on backroads
& cruise into Wingo, Kentucky,
population entirely in hiding.
Here we receive disconcerting
news. The casket shop has moved.
So says the only sign in town,
bolted to a windowless brick
building. Before we can find
the new casket shop, or anything
else, we're cruising out of Wingo,
at roughly the speed I've traveled
through most of my life. All those
breaths & hours, canyons of worry:
a puff of wind. Come my final hour,
I'll pass on a casket, thank you.
Pass also on one of those eco-
boxes that lets the earth have at
you in the sodden cardboard dark.
Give me high flower valleys, please.
Peaks of snowlit fire. Let my ashes
zephyr off while friends & family
lift their arms & sing
Wingo!
Wingo!
Wingo!

Acknowledgments

My hearty thanks to the following literary magazines where these poems first appeared, sometimes in slightly different form.

"Big Day," a finalist in *Terrain.org's* poetry contest judged by Ross Gay
"Circus Flyer"—*Booth*
"Reprieve"—*Non-Binary Review*
"The Darker Moods of My Father—*The Pinch*
"Windy Day at the Dump"—*Blue Earth Review*
"Depression (1): In the Snowy Range" appeared in my first poetry collection, *The Exact Weight of the Soul* (Santa Fe, 2020), Red Mountain Press

I'd like to thank the Muse, wherever she resides and by whatever mysteries she works, for continuing to keep me in her sights and for sparking the first image or draft of these poems. May I remain open to her gifts.

I write initially in a garret of my own making, sure, but soon enough I rely on the guidance, advice, and support of wonderful people. In the case of this book, first thanks to SueEllen Campbell, my wife and first editor, who among other important things knows when I'm writing like myself and when I am not.

Giant thanks to Susan Tichy, wonderful poet and teacher, firm but kind soul, who agreed to be my poetry mentor after I contacted her out of the blue, in my retirement—and in hers. She helped me in particular with two kinds of breaks, those of the poetic line and those that helped me to cut away from lazy habits of writing and mind, all the while offering me new visions of what a poem and poet can be.

Enduring thanks to my three-pack of workshop pals in poetry and life who have critiqued my work: Jack Martin, Steve Miles, Evan Oakley. Thanks to close readers and friends: Bill Tremblay, Steven Schwartz, Marj Hahne, Mark Easter, Ben Brown, Frank and Kathleen Dean Moore. My, have I been fortunate in my friendships.

Special thanks to generous and insightful Dan Beachy-Quick, who sat down with me several times to look at some of these poems.

I'm grateful to Dan, Ellie Waterston, and Michael Branch for kind words about this book.

Thanks to good-souled writers Peter Anderson, Art Goodtimes, and Lorrie Wolfe. Ditto my CSU and Fort Collins poet-colleagues, who have encouraged my late-life drift from nonfiction to poetry: Matthew Cooperman, Aby Kaupang, and Sasha Steenson.

Thanks, as always, to my friend, *Colorado Review* editor-*extraordinaire* Stephanie G'Schwind, for a hundred kindnesses, and to Arne G'Schwind, who helped me to record audios of some of these pieces.

Thanks to my hiking and talking pal, adventure writer Jim Davidson. Same for C.E. Janecek, editor and organizer, who has so skillfully submitted poems for me.

I'm grateful to talented photographer Phil Benstein, who generously allowed us to use his image of roseate spoonbills for the cover.

Finally, thank you, David Martin, for bringing out this and other handsome books with Middle Creek Publishing, and for the environmental and regional focus of your press.

About the Author

John Calderazzo's poems, essays, and literary journalism have appeared in *Audubon, Bellevue Literary Review, Brevity, Georgia Review, Orion, Terrain.org* and elsewhere. His first poetry collection is *The Exact Weight of the Soul* (Red Mountain Press, 2020). Among his three nonfiction books is *Rising Fire: Volcanoes & Our Inner Lives*. His work has appeared in many anthologies, including *Best American Nature Writing*, *Best Travel Adventure Stories,* and Copper Canyon Press's *Here: Poems for the Planet*. English Professor *Emeritus* at Colorado State University, he's won a Best CSU Teacher Award, a Colorado Council on the Arts Fellowship and founded the literary nonfiction track of the CSU Teacher awarded and a Colorado Council on the Arts Fellowship, and he founded the literary nonfictionCreative Writing program. Nowadays, he teaches scientists to use storytelling skills to communicate with the public and enjoys trekking among high mountains around the world.

About the Press

Middle Creek Publishing & Audio is a company seeking to make the world a better place through both the means and ends of publishing. We are publishers of quality literature in any genre from authors and artists, both seasoned and those who are undiscovered or under-valued, or under-represented, with a great interest in works which illuminate or embody any aspect of contemplative Human Ecology, defined as the relationship between humans and their natural, social, and built environments.

Middle Creek Publishing & Audio's particular interest in Human Ecology is meant to clarify an aspect of the quality in the works we will consider for publication and as a guide to those considering submitting work to us. Our interest is in publishing works which illuminate the human experience through words, story or other content that connects us to each other, our environment, our history, and our potential deeply and more consciously.

In 2025, we created a nonprofit, Middle Creek Press, an NTEE A33: Arts, Culture, and Humanities - Printing and Publishing nonprofit organization. Once we transfer all business and processes over, this will empower us to focus more on the quality of our work and extend our literary reach. Be part of this transformative journey by supporting our fundraising efforts. If you have a moment, drop us a line at:

middlecreekpublishing@outlook.com to give us feedback on our impact that we can use in grants reporting.

Charitable tax-deductible donations may be made now to:

Middle Creek Press
9161 Pueblo Mountain Park Road
Beulah, CO 81023

Middle Creek
Publishing

www.ingramcontent.com/pod-product-compliance
Lightning Source LLC
Chambersburg PA
CBHW080546090426
42734CB00016B/3219